BOOK ON SPACE:
ASTEROIDS AND METEORS

SPEEDY
PUBLISHING

Speedy Publishing LLC
40 E. Main St. #1156
Newark, DE 19711
www.speedypublishing.com

Every day, Earth is
bombarded with more
than 100 tons of dust
and sand-sized particles.

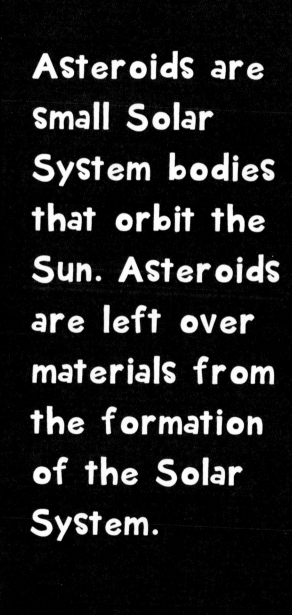

Asteroids are small Solar System bodies that orbit the Sun. Asteroids are left over materials from the formation of the Solar System.

Asteroids vary greatly in size, some feature diameters as small as ten metres while others stretch out over hundreds of kilometres.

The large majority of known asteroids orbit in the asteroid belt between the orbits of Mars and Jupiter.

Asteroids are
rich in precious
metals and
other metals, as
well as water.

A meteoroid
that burns up
as it passes
through
the Earth's
atmosphere
is known as
a meteor.

Millions of meteors occur in the Earth's atmosphere daily. Most meteoroids that cause meteors are about the size of a grain of sand.

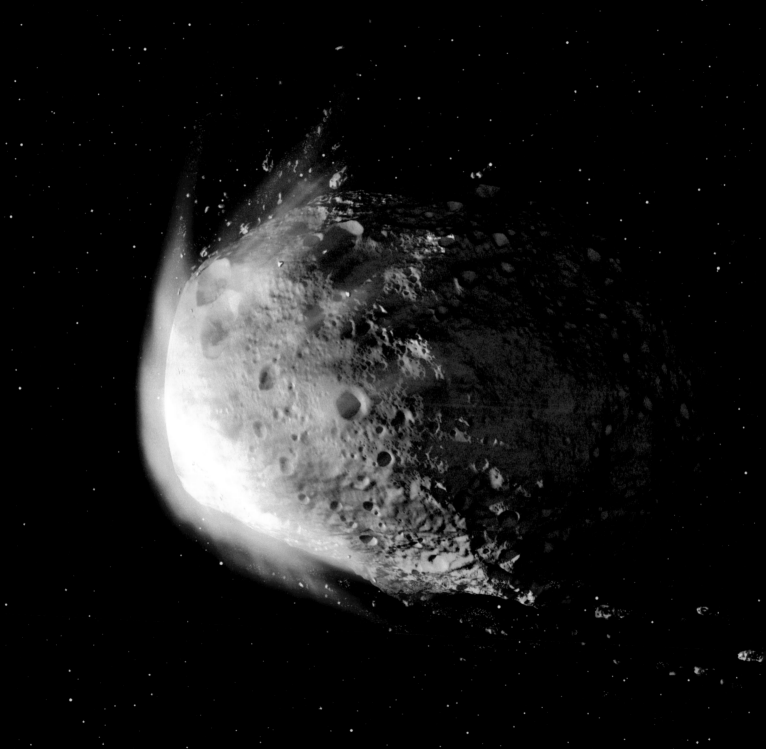

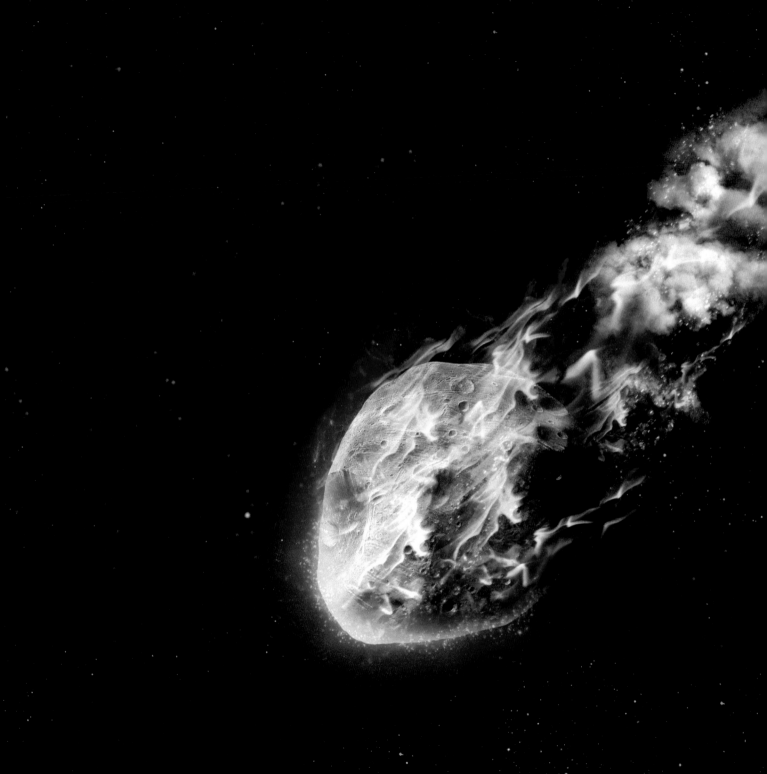

Meteors can travel as slow as 25,000 mph and reach speeds up to 160,000 miles per hour.

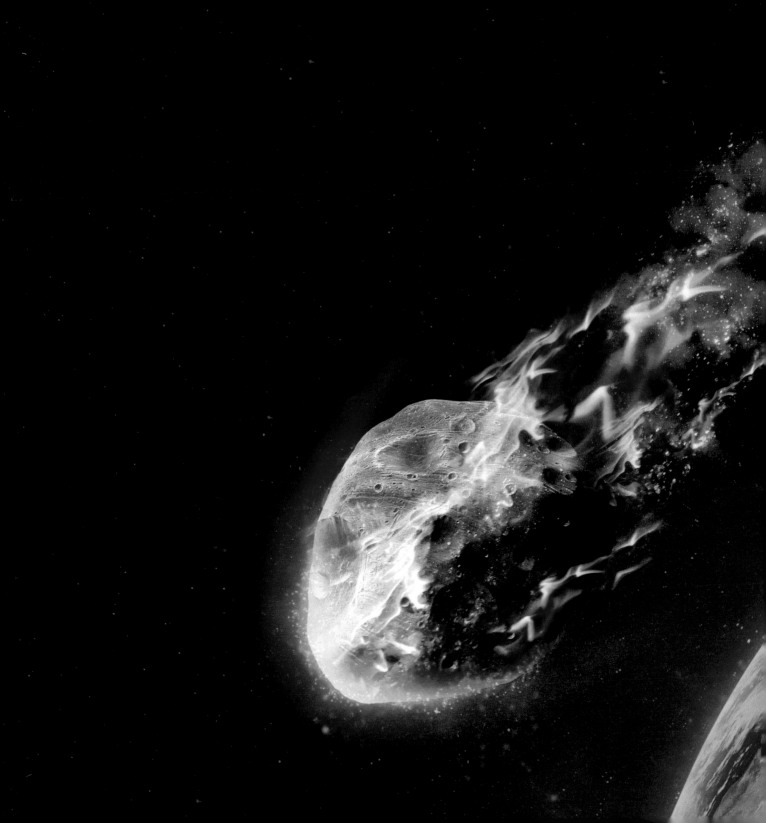

Made in the USA
Las Vegas, NV
21 November 2021

34962017R00021